W9-AOZ-112

Wonders of Nature
Waterfalls

Dana Meachen Rau

Marshall Cavendish
Benchmark
New York

2

Watch the water in a river. It moves quickly over rocks. It flows through the forest.

Sometimes a river comes to a *cliff*. The water keeps flowing.

It flows right over the edge and makes a waterfall.

Waterfalls happen when water moves from high ground to low ground. Waterfalls are often found in places with lots of mountains.

Water *erodes*, or changes, the land. Rivers carry dirt. Rivers make rocks smooth. Rivers even break off pieces of rock.

In some rivers, hard rock lies further up the river than soft rock. The water erodes the soft rock. The soft rock breaks away. This leaves a hard rock cliff for water to fall over.

The falling water keeps eroding the hard rock, too. Waterfalls move back little by little. Over many years, the waterfall moves further up the river.

Waterfalls can be small. The little waterfalls you see in a river are called *rapids*. They form when the water flows quickly over rocks.

Some people ride rapids
in *kayaks*.

Waterfalls can be tall. The tallest waterfall is Angel Falls. Angel Falls is in Venezuela, a country in South America.

Waterfalls can be wide. The widest waterfall is Victoria Falls. It is one mile wide. Victoria Falls is on the Zambezi River in Africa.

The Niagara River flows over cliffs between the United States and Canada. Niagara Falls is really two big waterfalls and one that is smaller. They are called the American Falls, the Horseshoe Falls, and the Bridal Veil Falls.

A big milk jug contains one *gallon*. About 600,000 gallons of water fall over Horseshoe Falls every second. That is a lot of jugs of water!

24

The bottom of a waterfall is often filled with rocks. Some of the rocks broke off from the cliff above. The water falling on the rocks makes a loud crashing sound.

Falling water is very powerful.
Some people use waterpower
to make machines work.

The running water moves parts of the machine.

Waterfalls make a *mist* that looks like smoke. If you are close enough, you might get sprayed with water. If the sun is shining, you might see a rainbow in the mist.

29

Challenge Words

cliff (KLIF)—A steep, rocky drop from high to low.

erodes (ee-ROHDS)—To wear away the land.

gallon (GAL-uhn)—A liquid measurement.

kayaks (KIE-aks)—Small boats covered all around except for an opening for a person to sit and paddle.

mist (MIST)—Very tiny drops of water in the air.

rapids (RAP-ids)—The part of a river where very fast-moving water flows over rocks.

Index

Page numbers in **boldface** are illustrations.

bottom, **24**, 25

cliffs, **4**, 4–5, **5**, 10, **11**, **24**, 25

erosion, **8**, 9–13, **12**

forming waterfalls, **4**, **5**, 6, **7**, 10, **11**

gallons, 22

land. *See* erosion

machines, 26–27, **27**
mist, 28, **29**
mountains, 6
moving waterfalls, **12**, 13

Niagara Falls, **20**, 21–22, **23**

people, 15, **15**, 26, 28
power, **26**, 26–27, **27**

rainbows, 28
rapids, **14**, 14–15, **15**
rivers, **2**, 3–5, **4**, **5**, **8**, 9–10, 14, **14**
rock(s), **2**, 3, 9–14, **24**, 25

size, **14**, 14–21, **16**, **19**
sound, 25

water
  amount of, 22
  flowing, **2**, 3–5, **4**, **5**, **26**, 26–27, **27**

With thanks to Nanci Vargus, Ed.D.,
and Beth Walker Gambro, reading consultants

Marshall Cavendish Benchmark
99 White Plains Road
Tarrytown, New York 10591-9001
www.marshallcavendish.us

Library of Congress Cataloging-in-Publication Data

Rau, Dana Meachen, 1971–
Waterfalls / by Dana Meachen Rau.
p. cm. — (Bookworms. Wonders of nature)
Summary: "Provides a basic introduction to waterfalls,
including geographical information and how they are formed"—Provided by publisher.
Includes index.
ISBN 978-0-7614-2671-4
1. Waterfalls—Juvenile literature. I. Title. II. Series.
GB1403.8.R38 2007
551.48'4—dc22
2006038620

Editor: Christina Gardeski
Publisher: Michelle Bisson
Designer: Virginia Pope
Art Director: Anahid Hamparian

Photo Research by Anne Burns Images

Cover Photo by *Corbis*/Free Agents Limited

The photographs in this book are used with permission and through the courtesy of:
Photo Researchers: pp. 1, 12 David R. Frazier; p. 2 Byron Jorjorian; p. 8 George Ranalli; p. 14 Michael Lustbader;
p. 26 Science Source. *Corbis*: p. 4 Joseph Sohm/ChromoSohm Inc.; p. 5 Paul Hardy; p. 11 Paul Souders;
pp. 15, 19 Royalty Free; p. 23 Ron Watts; p. 24 Bill Ross; p. 27 Massimo Borchi; p. 29 James Randklev.
Peter Arnold: p. 7 Jeremy Woodhouse/WW1; p. 16 Kevin Schafer; p. 20 Jeff Greenberg.

Printed in Malaysia

j551.48   Rau, Dana Meachen.
RAU
          Waterfalls.

j551.48   Rau, Dana
RAU   Meachen.

          Waterfalls.

$22.79

DATE	BORROWER'S NAME		

48109

DISCARD